Kokuteeru

Mr. Yonekichi Maeda
(Printed with permission from the Maeda family)

Kokuteeru

by
Yonekichi Maeda

Translated by
Kagumi Otani

Introduction to this edition by
Eiji Arakawa

MIXELLANY

Email: mixellanyltd@googlemail.com

Text & Cover design: Lynda Mills

First edition

British Library Cataloguing in Publication Data Available

ISBN: 978-1-907434-60-0 (hardcover);

ISBN: 978-1-907434-61-7 (tradepaper);

ISBN: 978-1-907434-62-4 (deluxe edition)

$\mathcal{C}$ontents

Mr. Maeda in front of his parent's house in Kagoshima pref. Japan. It is believed that the person sitting in the chair next to him may be his newlywed wife, Yuwa.
(Printed with permission from the Maeda family)

Mr. Maeda with friends on the opening day of his own liquor store, circa late 1920s. (Printed with permission from the Maeda family)

Translator's Note

When I opened *Kokuteeru* for the first time and gave it a quick read, my initial thought was 'oh my god what have I got myself into?'

Firstly, it was all written in old Japanese which is quite different from how it is now. Secondly it was written as how it sounded to the author Yonekichi Maeda.

As "cocktail" does not sound like "kokuteeru" to me, it was almost like solving the puzzle created by him, trying to get into his mind. As far as I go, my mind was blown by this man. How the hell did he manage to write this amazing cocktail book in 1920s Japan? No way he knew so many bloody cool Martini-twists!

Later, I learnt that there is a theory that he might have worked as a cook or waiter on a navy ship and that was how he met people from all over the world and was shared the cocktail recipes by them.

I cannot help myself trying to imagine how cool and interesting it was for him to experience that, how many drunken nights they had (hmm jealous). Also, it seemed like this legend was friends with Masataka Taketsuru, known by Nikka Taketsuru—Pure malt; who also was featured in a TV series in Japan a few years ago and it was a huge hit. How come Yonekichi Maeda never saw the light of day? Well, it looks like the time has come. It is an honour to be part of this process, to be able to assist sending this amazing book to the world after 100 YEARS! Enjoy, try some recipes & get tipsy.

—Kagumi Otani

Mr. Maeda in full costume. In front of the entrance of his own liquor store.
(Printed with permission from the Maeda family)

Introduction to the 2022 Reprint of *Kokuteeru*

The cocktail was first introduced to Japan about 160 years ago, shortly after the opening of the country to the outside world at the end of the Edo period (1603–1868). The first bar in Japan opened in the Yokohama Hotel in the foreign settlement of Yokohama in 1860, followed half a century later in 1910 by the first street bar in Tokyo, Café Printemps, in Ginza, Tokyo. During this period, coupled with the atmosphere of "Taisho democracy," cafés and bars opened one after another in major cities.

In 1924, the first two cocktail books were published by Japanese authors. One was *Cocktails: How To Mix Drinks?*" by Tokuzo Akiyama, and the other, *Kokuteeru* (Cocktails) by Yonekichi Maeda (1897-1939), which was published a month after Akiyama's book.

While Mr. Akiyama was a prominent figure, who served Emperor Taisho (and later Emperor Showa) as the head chef, Mr. Yonekichi Maeda was just 27 years old at the time and an unknown bartender working at a restaurant called Café Line in Yotsuya, Tokyo. Whereas Akiyama's book described how to make individual cocktails entirely in text, Maeda's book systematically introduced 298 cocktails, with recipes listed as "***** one-half, ****** one-third, *****".

The design was so practical that Maeda's book must have been more useful for professional bartenders at the time. One can imagine that it must have been quite a challenge to write such a highly accomplished book at a time when information on Western liquors and cocktails was scarce.

Curiously, *Kokuteeru* contains some 30 cocktails that would appear in print for the first time in the Europe in *The Savoy Cocktail Book* (1930), a historical classic that was published six years later. Among them are cocktails are clearly original to the author, Harry Craddock. This is a great mystery, and it is very intriguing to know how Mr. Maeda came across the recipes six years before the publication of the Savoy book in faraway Japan, far away in the East.

Unfortunately, *Kokuteeru* went out of print in the pre-war (the World War II) days and is now a hard-to-find book. I thought to myself, "It would be a shame for its valuable contents to remain out of the light of day. I wanted to introduce its contents to today's bartenders as well," and recently I was able to reprint the book in its entirety on my blog with commentary in serial form (February–May 2011).

One day, about six years after the serialization, an unexpected stroke of good fortune came my way: a descendant of Yonekichi Maeda (though not a direct descendant), his niece Kayoko Maeda (aged 76) and her eldest son Hideki (aged 46), who saw my article on the website, contacted me directly. (Without the

Internet invention, such a happy encounter would not have been possible.)

I was able to hear valuable and interesting stories and information about the late Mr. Maeda, whose career was almost a mystery to us. To our delight, we also received some rare and previously unpublished photos of Mr. Maeda who was born in Kagoshima Prefecture in 1897 and moved to Tokyo by 1921. But the only information we have about his career before he started working at Café Line is that he was probably working in the restaurant and bar industry.

How did Mr. Maeda come to know about the latest cocktail information from Europe? Of course, it is possible that Mr. Maeda, who was working in the food and beverage industry in Tokyo around 1921, could have obtained information about this and that directly from foreigners who visited Tokyo. He may have had access to the Savoy Hotel's drink menu and recipes in some way.

However, one of the previously undisclosed photos they brought to me offered a surprising clue that may lead to the answer. It is a commemorative photo of Mr. Maeda, dressed in a stylish white suit, holding what appears to be a framed letter of appreciation with some sort of inscription. The photo shows an old Navy warship. The Navy often sent its fleet to Europe on "goodwill visits" during this period, although the timing is unclear.

I imagine that Mr. Maeda may have been asked to accompany a Navy warship on a goodwill visit to Europe for some reason, and that he was asked to serve food and drinks during the voyage. We do not know the name of the ship or the port of call at this time, but it is quite probable that he may have obtained the latest local information (recipes), including the bar at the Savoy Hotel, in some way during his port of call in England... and so on.

After publishing *Kokuteeru*, Mr. Maeda retired from Café Line and opened his own liquor store, Maeda Yonekichi Honten in Ginza at the beginning of the Showa period (1926-1989). He sold not only Western liquors but also bottled cocktails, and apparently had business with the venerable Mitsukoshi Department Store. Unfortunately, he passed away suddenly in 1939 at the age of 42.

Many of the standard cocktails featured in contemporary cocktail books were created during the 1910s-1930s, while Mr. Maeda was struggling with cocktails. And now, 100 years later, classic cocktails from the olden days are being reevaluated and revisited in bars in major cities around the world. The new original cocktails created every day are also the result of efforts of our predecessors. *Kokuteeru* reminds me once again of the importance of learning from the past.

The mystery surrounding *Kokuteeru* and Mr. Yonekichi Maeda has yet to be solved. Above all, many mysteries remain in relation to the Savoy Hotel (Savoy Cocktail Book). This book is a valuable record of the "first steps" taken by a pioneer of the Japanese bar industry, who began his walk with the hope of spreading Western cocktail culture. In the near future, we may be able to discover Mr. Maeda's precious cocktail notebooks and other materials from that time...

I sincerely hope that my dream comes true someday.

—Eiji Arakawa Cocktail Historian
Owner-bartender/Bar UK, Osaka, Japan

コクテール

著者　前田米吉

カフエ、ライン藏版

Introduction by Yoshi Amakusa
(1924)

Cocktails started in Tokyo soon after the War. Cocktails are a new type of beverage that are served to many customers in social occasions however after the Kanto earth quake disaster, they disappeared for a while as they were not essential items in everyone's life.

Recovery from the natural disaster progressed gradually in Tokyo and we were happy to see the culture of cocktail start coming back. While hard work is required by everyone, including myself, for recovery from the large natural disaster, I don't think feeling sad about our current life being so hard helps the recovery of one's life.

That is not what we need in Tokyo nor Japan now. I believe people in Tokyo need hope and positive energy, they need to work hard and eat well rather than feeling sad about what has happened. I believe sharing the experience of drinking cocktails with others can bring positivity for the future, to help us to live stronger tomorrow & contribute to creating a better life in our society.

The Cocktail started about 100 years ago in a city of Ireland with a wealthy man who had a very good fighting rooster and a very beautiful young daughter. She was so beautiful that she kept receiving marriage requests. However, she was very obedient to her father and was never interested in accepting any of those marriage requests. She was very happy keeping herself busy with house work. One day his precious rooster had gone missing. Everyone in his family went out and looked for it everywhere but no one could find the rooster. Evening came and rooster still did not come home. The next morning, the man left home to look for his rooster. He travelled far and everywhere and asked everyone about his prize rooster but the rooster could not be found. He came back home with a broken heart and fell ill. His daughter was so worried she suggested to him that she would get married with the man who brings his rooster back home. This suggestion brought him joy so he placed advertisements in all the local newspapers proclaiming that the man who returns his rooster would be able to marry his daughter.

A few days later, a soldier on his horse came to the wealthy man's gate and requested to see the master. As the man was not well and in bed, his beautiful daughter came out to meet the soldier instead. When she saw the soldier, she lost her words as he was the most handsome noble man. And the soldier also lost his words and could not help but to stare at her beauty. After a moment, he brought out something from the back of his cape – it was her father's precious rooster! The daughter run to her father's bedroom and told him that the soldier had found his rooster and brought it home. Her father jumped out from the bed and ran to his rooster, scooping it up with joy. He shook the soldier's hand and thanked him and approved his daughter to marry the soldier. The father told his daughter to pour a celebration drink for them. His daughter's hands were shaking with joy and could not pay attention to the bottles she was pouring into the glasses and ended up mixing whatever she could into their glasses. Both the soldier and her father were so happy and toasted to their future with the mixed drinks. This randomly mixed drink tasted so good and they enjoyed it so much they all began to tell people about the drink. The story became popular among the soldiers and they named the drink Cocktail (rooster's tail). As time goes on, Cocktails became popular and got improved with different flavours and recipes. Based on the story, tradition was made for male patrons to start drinking cocktails before female patrons in social gathering.

When making the cocktails in this book ratios are based on 70% capacity of a cocktail glass (1 oz). Ingredients are mixed either in a shaker or in a mixing glass. When pouring into the glass, along with melted ice and maraschino cherry etc, it should fill about 80% of the cocktail glass. When mixing 2-3 servings of cocktail, simply change amount of the ingredients accordingly. A drop is the same amount of 2-3 drops come out of a straw. Using the Base part of cocktail shaker as a mixing glass is easy and practical. You can use anything as cocktail tools and glasses as long as they are maintained well and kept cleaned all times. Don't be a lazy bartender who has expensive tools but does not know how to look after them. Cocktails requires certain ingredients and flavours, they require good balance to create a good drink with good flavour. If there is not good balance then the drink will not be good. It also requires skills while shaking and mixing. If the bar does not have skilled bartenders, you cannot make customers happy. As cocktail culture is still new it has been difficult to have all required ingredients to carry out studies to improve our cocktails. I feel very fortunate and wish to celebrate as I publish this book which was created by the support of many Café owners and people who enjoy making cocktails at home along with the very experienced Mr. Maeda. I hope this will become a good guide to all the bartenders, and as a bartender, I wish to receive any feedback about this book.

October 1924
Café Line Owner
Yoshi Amakusa

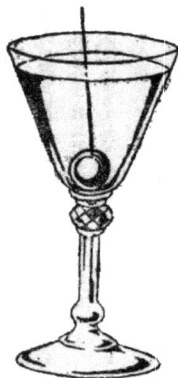

*Mr. Maeda with a framed letter of appreciation,
taken in the early 1920s.
(Printed with permission from the Maeda family)*

Main Ingredients
Spirits, Liquor, Tools

.... French Vermouth ....

.... Italian Vermouth ....

.... Scotch whisky ....

.... Brandy ....

.... Peach Brandy ....

.... Apricot Brandy ....

.... Cherry Brandy ....

.... Dom Benedictine ....

.... Dry Gin ....

.... Old Tom Gin ....

.... Sloe Gin ....

.... Orange Curacao ....

.... White Curacao ....

.... Vodka ....

.... Crème de Cacao ....

.... Crème de Violet ....

.... Chartreuse Green ....

.... Chartreuse Yellow ....

.... Mandarin ....

.... Maraschino ....

.... Anisette ....

.... Bols Kummel ....

.... Picon Amer ....

.... Mèdoc ....

.... Line Wine ....

.... Madeira ....

.... Sherry ....

.... Jamaican Rum ....

.... Port wine ....

.... White Port ....

.... Maraschino Cherry ....

.... Soda Water ....

.... Olive ....

.... Champagne ....

.... Orange Bitter ....

.... Angostura Bitter ....

.... Pepper Mint ....

.... Orgeat ....

.... Syrup ....

.... Lime juice ....

.... Grape juice ...

.... Ginger ale ...

.... Mitsuya Cider ...

著者
Author

英國型　　　　　　　　　独逸型

コクテールセーカー

English Style　　　　　　　German Style

Cocktail Shakers

24

Punch Glass	Champagne Glass	Water Glass
チ ン ボ スラグ	ンペンヤシ スラグ	ータスオウ スラグ

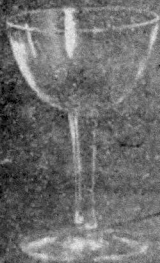

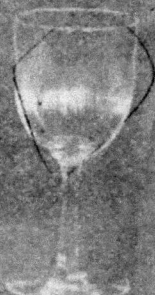

ルーテクコ スラグ	ーユキリ スラグ	ー リ セ スラグ	ンイワトーボ スラグ
Cocktail Glass	Liquor Glass	Sherry Glass	Port Wine Glass

List of Cocktails

Cocktails

Punch

Rickey

Cup

Lemonade

Cooler

Crusta

Fizz

Flip

$\mathcal{P}$ousse-cafe

$\mathcal{C}$obbler

$\mathcal{E}$ggnog

$\mathcal{D}$aisy

$\mathcal{S}$our

$\mathcal{J}$ulep

$\mathcal{S}$ling

$\mathcal{O}$thers

Cocktails

Inca Cocktail

Orgeat Syrup	2 dash
Orange Bitter	2 dash
Plymouth Gin	1/3 oz
French Vermouth	1/3 oz
Dry Sherry	1/3 oz

Add all the ingredients into a mixing glass half-filled with crushed ice, stir well, strain into a cocktail glass. Garnish with a piece of pineapple and some lemon peel.

Immutable Cocktail

Sugar	1/2 tsp
Angostura Bitter	1 dash
Old Tom or Dry Gin	1 oz

Add all the ingredients into a cocktail glass with one piece of ice, add some lemon peel and stir.

India Cocktail

Angostura bitters	1 dash
Curacao	1 dash
Maraschino	1 dash
Brandy	1 oz

Add all the ingredients into a cocktail glass with a small ice cube. Squeeze a wedge of lemon and stir.

Ades Cocktail

Angostura Bitter............ 1 dash
Absinthe .... 1/3 oz
Anisette......................... 1/3 oz

Add all the ingredients in a cocktail shaker with 3 pieces of ice and shake well, pour into a cocktail glass. Garnish with a piece of pineapple.

London Cocktail

Orange bitter .... 1 dash
Gomme Syrup............... 1 dash
Absinthe . ... 1 dash
London Dry Gin........... 1 oz

Add all the ingredients in a mixing glass half-filled with crushed ice, stir well and strain into a cocktail glass. Garnish with an olive and some lemon peel.

Lone Tree Cocktail

Old Tom or Dry Gin.... 1 oz
French Vermouth.......... small amount

Add both of the ingredients in a cocktail shaker and shake lightly, Strain into a cocktail glass.

Rob Roy Cocktail

Curacao	1 or 2 dash
Angostura bitter	1 dash
Rye Whisky	½ oz
French Vermouth	½ oz

Add all the ingredients in a mixing glass half-filled with crushed ice, Stir well and strain into a cocktail glass. Garnish with a maraschino cherry and some lemon peel.

Rossington Cocktail

Orange Juice	small amount
Cinzano Vermouth	1/3 oz
Gordon Dry Gin	1/3 oz

Add all the ingredients into a cocktail shaker with 2-3 pieces of ice and shake well, pour into a cocktail glass. Garnish with some orange peel.

Royale Cocktail

Orange Bitter	1 dash
Angostura Bitter	1 dash
Old Tom Gin	1/3 oz
Dubonnet	1/3 oz

Add all the ingredients in a mixing glass half-filled with crushed ice, stir well and strain into a cocktail glass. Garnish with a maraschino cherry and some lemon peel.

Long Range Cocktail

Gomme syrup	1 dash
Angostura Bitter	2 dash
Italian Vermouth	2/5 oz
Absinthe	2/5 oz
Brandy	1/5 oz

Add all of the ingredients into a cocktail shaker with 2-3 pieces of ice and shake well. Rub the inside of a cocktail glass with lemon peel, pour the cocktail into the glass and garnish with some lemon peel.

Los Cocktail

Grenadine	2 dash
Dry Gin	2/4 oz
French Vermouth	1/4 oz
Dubonnet	1/4 oz

Add all the ingredients into a mixing glass half-filled with crushed ice and stir well, strain into a cocktail glass. Garnish with a maraschino cherry and some lemon peel.

Harvard Cocktail

Angostura Bitter	1 dash
Gomme Syrup	1 dash
Brandy	1/2 oz
Italian Vermouth	1/2 oz

Add all the ingredients into a mixing glass half-filled with crushed ice and stir well, strain into a cocktail glass. Garnish with some lemon peel.

Harlem Cocktail

       Orange Bitter.................2 dash
       Italian Vermouth...........1/3 oz
       Whisky.............................2/3 oz

Add all the ingredients into a cocktail shaker with 2-3 pieces of ice, shake well and pour into a cocktail glass. Garnish with a maraschino cherry.

Handicap Cocktail

       Grand Marnier ....1 oz
       Mitsuya Lemon-lime Cider   175ml
       (half of bottle)

Add both of the ingredients into a mixing glass half-filled with crushed ice, stir quietly and pour into a wine glass. Garnish with some lemon peel.

Hula Cocktail

       Orange Juice ....1/3 oz
       Curacao...........................1/2 tsp
       Dry Gin...........................2/3 oz

Add all the ingredients into a cocktail shaker with 2-3 pieces of ice, shake well and pour into a cocktail glass.

Palmetto Cocktail

Orange Bitter.. ....2 dash
Jamaica Rum....................1/2 dash
Italian Vermouth............1/2 dash

Add all the ingredients into a mixing glass half-filled
with crushed ice, stir well and strain into a cocktail
glass. Garnish with some lemon peel.

Holland Cocktail

Angostura Bitter.............2 dash
Gomme Syrup................1 dash
Holland Gin ....1 oz

Add all the ingredients into a cocktail shaker with
2-3 pieces of ice and shake well, strain into a cocktail
glass. Garnish with a maraschino cherry.

Paradise Cocktail

Orange Juice ....1/3 oz
Apricot Brandy...............1/3 oz
Dry Gin ....1/3 oz

Add all the ingredients into a cocktail shaker with 2-3
pieces of ice, shake well and pour into a cocktail glass.

Perfect Cocktail

Old Tom or Dry Gin....1/3 oz
Italian Vermouth...........1/3 oz
French Vermouth..........1/3 oz

Add all the ingredients into a mixing glass half-filled with crushed ice and stir well, strain into a cocktail glass. Garnish with some lemon peel.

Bamboo Cocktail

Orange Bitter.................1 dash
Dry Sherry ....1/2 oz
French Vermouth..........1/2 oz

Add all the ingredients into a mixing glass half-filled with crushed ice and stir well, strain into a cocktail glass. Garnish with some lemon peel.

Bacardi Cocktail

Lime Juice ....3-4 dash
Bacardi...........................1 oz

Add both of the ingredients into a mixing glass half-filled with crushed ice and stir, gradually add sugar syrup until it meets the desired sweetness. Strain into a cocktail glass and garnish with some lemon peel.

Nick's Own Cocktail

Angostura Bitter	1 dash
Absinthe	1 dash
Brandy	1/2 oz
Italian Vermouth	1/2 oz

Add all the ingredients into a mixing glass half-filled with crushed ice and stir well, strain into a cocktail glass. Garnish with a maraschino cherry and some lemon peel.

Honolulu Cocktail

Sugar	1 tsp
Lemon Juice	1/2 lemon
Angostura Bitter	2 dash
Curacao	2 dash
Egg White	1 egg
Dry Gin	1/3 oz
Orange Juice	1/4 oz

Add all the ingredients into a mixing glass half-filled with crushed ice, stir well strain into a wine glass.

White Cocktail

Angostura Bitter	1 dash
Anisette	1 dash
Dry Gin	1oz

Add all the ingredients into a mixing glass half-filled with crushed ice and stir well, strain into a cocktail glass. Garnish with an olive and some lemon peel.

Boomerang Cocktail

Maraschino	1 dash
Angostura Bitter	1 dash
Gin	1/3 oz
Italian Vermouth	1/3 oz
French Vermouth	1/3 oz

Add all the ingredients into a mixing glass half-filled with crushed ice and stir well, strain into a cocktail glass. Garnish with a maraschino cherry and some lemon peel.

Perfecto Cocktail

Gordon Dry Gin	4/6 oz
French Vermouth	1/6 oz
Italian Vermouth	1/6 oz
Absinthe	1 dash

Add all the ingredients into a cocktail shaker with 2-3 pieces of ice and shake well, pour into a cocktail glass. Garnish with some orange peel.

Bennett Cocktail

Angostura Bitter	1 dash
Old Tom Gin	1 oz
Lime Juice	small amount

Add all the ingredients into a cocktail shaker with 2-3 pieces of ice and shake well, pour into a cocktail glass.

Vermouth Cocktail

Angostura Bitter.............3 dash
Italian Vermouth...........1 oz
French Vermouth..........small amount

Add all the ingredients into a mixing glass half-filled with crushed ice and still well, strain into a cocktail glass. Garnish with an olive.

Trocadero Cocktail

Orange Bitter_................1 dash
Grenadine...... ....1 dash
French Vermouth..........1/2 oz
Italian Vermouth...........1/2 oz

Add all the ingredients into a mixing glass half-filled with crushed ice and stir well, strain into a cocktail glass. Garnish with a maraschino cherry and some lemon peel.

Tom Gin Cocktail

Orange Bitter.................1 dash
Maraschino.. ....1 dash
Old Tom Gin.................1 oz

Add all the ingredients into a mixing glass half-filled with crushed ice and stir well, strain into a cocktail glass. Garnish with some lemon peel.

Doctor Cocktail

Lemon Juice	1/6 oz
Orange Juice	1/6 oz
Caloric Punch	4/6 oz

Add all the ingredients into a cocktail shaker and shake well, pour into a cocktail glass.

Thistle Cocktail

Angostura Bitter	1 dash
Italian Vermouth	1/3 oz
Rye Whisky	2/3 oz

Add all the ingredients into a mixing glass half filled with crushed ice and stir well, strain into a cocktail glass. Garnish with some lemon peel.

Chinese Cocktail

Angostura Bitter	1 dash
Maraschino	2 dash
Curacao	2 dash
Grenadine	2 dash
Jamaica Rum	1 oz

Add all the ingredients into a mixing glass half-filled with crushed ice and stir well, pour into a cocktail glass. Garnish with a maraschino cherry and some lemon peel.

Tipperary Cocktail

Orange Juice	1/2 tsp
Grenadine	1/2 tsp
Mint	2 leaves
Italian Vermouth	1/3 oz
Gin	2/3 oz

Add all the ingredients into a cocktail shaker with 2-3 pieces of ice and shake well, pour into a cocktail glass.

Tuxedo No.2 Cocktail

Maraschino	1-2 dash
Orange Bitter	1 dash
Barnet Gin	1/2 oz
French Vermouth	1/2 oz
Absinthe	1 dash

Add all the ingredients into a mixing glass half- filled with crushed ice and stir well, strain into a cocktail glass. Garnish with lemon peel.

Chocolate Cocktail

Egg Yolk	1 egg
Yellow Chartreuse	1/2 oz
Port Wine	1/2 oz
Chocolate Powder	1/2 tsp

Add all the ingredients into a cocktail shaker with 2-3 pieces of ice and shake well, pour into a wine glass.

Luigi Cocktail

Grenadine........................1/2 tsp
Cointreau........................very small amount
Mandarin juice ....1/2 Mandarin
Gin ....1/2 oz
French Vermouth..........1/2 oz

Add all the ingredients into a cocktail shaker with 2-3 pieces of ice and shake well, pour into a cocktail glass.

Liberal Cocktail

Mandarin Juice...............4-5 drops
Picon Amer.....................2-3 drops
Whisky.............................1 oz

Add all the ingredients into a mixing glass half-filled with crushed ice and stir well, strain into a cocktail glass. Garnish with lemon peel.

Olivette Cocktail

Orange Bitter.................1 dash
Gomme Syrup...............1 dash
Absinthe.........................1 dash
Plymouth Gin...............1 oz Liberal Cocktail

Add all the ingredients into a mixing glass half-filled with crushed ice and stair well, strain into a cocktail glass. Garnish with an olive and some lemon peel.

Orange Blossom Cocktail

Orange Bitter........................1 dash
Grenadine...........................small amount
Orange Juice ....1/2 oz
Gin ....1/2 oz

Add all the ingredients into a cocktail shaker with 2-3 pieces of ice and shake well, pour into a cocktail glass.

Wax Cocktail

Orange Bitter........................2 dash
Plymouth Gin........................1 oz

Add both of the ingredients into a mixing glass half-filled with crushed ice and stir well, strain into a cocktail glass. Garnish with a maraschino cherry and some orange peel.

Cascarilla Cocktail

Cascarilla............................1/2 oz
Rye Whisky ....1/2 oz

Add both of the ingredients into a mixing glass half-filled with crushed ice and stir well, strain into a cocktail glass. Garnish with some lemon peel.

Coffee Cocktail

Egg Yolk.........................1 egg
Sugar Syrup...................1/2 tsp
Brandy............................1/2 oz
Port Wine......................1 oz

Add all the ingredients into a cocktail shaker with 2-3 pieces of ice and shake well, pour into a cocktail glass. Garnish with nutmeg powder.

Country Cocktail

Angostura Bitter............2 dash
Orange Bitter.................3 dash
Whisky............................1 oz

Add all the ingredients into a mixing glass half-filled with crushed ice and stir well, strain into a cocktail glass. Garnish with some lemon peel.

Canadian Cocktail

Gomme Syrup...............2 dash
Angostura Bitter............2 dash
Canadian Club...............1 oz
Italian Vermouth...........small amount

Add all the ingredients into a mixing glass half-filled with crushed ice and stir well, strain into a cocktail glass. Garnish with a maraschino cherry.

York Cocktail

Orange Bitter	2 dash
Whisky	2/3 oz
Italian Vermouth	1/3 oz

Add all the ingredients into a mixing glass half-filled with crushed ice and stir well, strain into a cocktail glass.

Turkish Cocktail

Orange Bitter	2 dash
Angostura Bitter	2 dash
French Vermouth	1/3 oz
Dry Gin	2/3 oz

Add all the ingredients into a mixing glass half-filled with crushed ice and stir well. Strain into a cocktail glass and add few drops of absinthe.

Tuxedo Cocktail

Angostura Bitter	1 dash
Sherry	small amount
Gin	1/2 oz
Italian Vermouth	1/2 oz

Add all the ingredients into a cocktail shaker with 2-3 pieces of ice and shake well, pour into a cocktail glass.

Tango Cocktail

Orange Bitter	4 dash
Gomme Syrup	3 dash
Vodka	1/3 oz
Gin	2/3 oz
Lemon Juice	1/4 oz
Egg White	1 egg

Add all the ingredients into a mixing glass and add small amount of soda water, stir well until it's foamy. Pour into a champagne glass.

Turf Cocktail

Orange Bitter	1 dash
Maraschino	1 dash
Absinthe	1 dash
Plymouth Gin	1/2 oz
French Vermouth	1/2 oz

Add all the ingredients into a mixing glass half-filled with crushed ice and stir well, strain into a cocktail glass. Garnish with an olive and some lemon peel.

Daiquiri Cocktail

Grenadine syrup	small amount
Lime Juice	1/3 oz
Bacardi	2/3 oz

Add all the ingredients into a cocktail shaker with 2-3 pieces of ice and shake well, pour into a cocktail glass.

$\mathcal{D}$empsey Cocktail

Absinthe	1 dash
Grenadine Syrup	1/2 tsp
Gin	1/3 oz
Calvados	2/3 oz

Add all the ingredients into a cocktail shaker with 2-3 pieces of ice and shake well, pour into a cocktail glass.

$\mathcal{D}$iki-Diki Cocktail

Calvados	3/5 oz
Caloric punch	1/5 oz
Grapefruit Juice	1/5 oz

Add all the ingredients into a cocktail shaker with 2-3 pieces of ice and shake well, pour into a cocktail glass.

$\mathcal{R}$aymond Hitch Cocktail

Orange Bitter	1 dash
Lemon Juice	¼ lemon
Pineapple	one small piece
Italian Vermouth	1 oz

Add all the ingredients into a cocktail shaker with 2-3 pieces of ice and shake well, pour into a cocktail glass.

Soda Cocktail

Sugar	2 tsp
Ice	1-2 pieces
Angostura Bitter	2 dash

Add all the ingredients into a soda glass, add some lemon peel and top up with cold water.

Line Cocktail

Angostura Bitter	2 dash
Benedictine	1/3 oz
Italian Vermouth	1/3 oz
Gin	1/3 oz

Add all the ingredients into a cocktail shaker with 2-3 pieces of ice and shake well. Pour into a cocktail glass and add some crushed Rakyyo (pickled shallot).

Racquet Club Cocktail

Orange Bitter	2 dash
Dry Gin	1/2 oz
French Vermouth	1/2 oz

Add all the ingredients into a mixing glass half-filled with crushed ice and stir well, strain into a cocktail glass. Garnish with some lemon peel.

Whiz Bang Cocktail

Orange Bitter..	1 dash
Grenadine	1 dash
Absinthe	1 dash
French Vermouth	1/3 oz
Scotch Whisky	2/3 oz

Add all the ingredients into a mixing glass half-filled with crushed ice and stir well, strain into a cocktail glass. Garnish with some lemon peel.

Ward Eight Cocktail

Grenadine	1/2 tsp
Orange Juice	1/4 oz
Lemon Juice	1/4 oz
Whisky	2/4 oz

Add all the ingredients into a cocktail shaker with 2-3 pieces of ice and shake well, pour into a cocktail glass.

Whisky Cocktail

Gomme Syrup	2 dash
Angostura Bitters	1 dash
Whisky	1 oz
Italian Vermouth	small amount
French Vermouth	small amount

Add all the ingredients into a cocktail shaker with 2-3 pieces of ice and shake well, pour into a cocktail glass. Garnish with a maraschino cherry.

Whip Cocktail

Absinthe Pernod	1/4 oz
French Vermouth	1/4 oz
Brandy	1/4 oz
Curacao	1/4 oz

Add all the ingredients into a cocktail shaker with 2-3 pieces of ice and shake well, pour into a cocktail glass.

Velocity Cocktail

Gin	2/3 oz
Orange	1 small piece
Italian Vermouth	1/3 oz

Add all the ingredients into a cocktail shaker with 2-3 pieces of ice and shake well, pour into a cocktail glass.

Vanderbilt Cocktail

Gomme Syrup	1-2 dash
Angostura Bitter	1 dash
Old Brandy	1/2 oz
Cherry Brandy	1/2 oz

Add all the ingredients into a mixing glass half-filled with crushed ice and stir well, strain into a cocktail glass. Garnish with a maraschino cherry and some lemon peel.

Queens Cocktail

Orange	1 small piece
Pineapple	1 small piece
Gin	1/3 oz
French Vermouth	1/3 oz
Italian Vermouth	1/3 oz

Add all the ingredients into a cocktail shaker with 2-3 pieces of ice and shake well, pour into a cocktail glass.

Cooperstown Cocktail

Orange Bitter	1 dash
Martini & Rossi Vermouth	1/3 oz
Gordon Fry Gin	2/3 oz
Mint	2-3 leaves

Add all the ingredients into a mixing glass half-filled with crushed ice and stir well, strain into a cocktail glass. Garnish with some lemon peel.

Club Cocktail

Angostura Bitter	1 dash
Grenadine.	1 dash
Canadian Club	1oz

Add all the ingredients into a mixing glass half-filled with crushed ice and stir well, strain into a cocktail glass. Garnish with a maraschino cherry and some lemon peel.

Crimson Cocktail

Orange Bitter	3 dash
Italian Vermouth	1/3 oz
Gin	2/3 oz

Add all the ingredients into a cocktail shaker with 2-3 pieces of ice and shake well, pour into a cocktail glass. Garnish with some lemon peel.

Klondike Cocktail

Orange Bitter	2 dash
French Vermouth	1/2 oz
Apple Jack Brandy	1/2 oz

Add all the ingredients into a mixing glass half-filled with crushed ice and stir well, strain into a cocktail glass. Garnish with an olive and some lemon peel.

Clover Club

Egg White	1 Egg
Grenadine	1/2 tsp
Gin	2/3 oz
French Vermouth	1/3 oz
Lime Juice	small amount

Add all the ingredients into a cocktail shaker with 2-3 pieces of ice and shake well, pour into a cocktail glass or wine glass.

Grade A Cocktail

Absinthe Pernod	2/3 oz
Pepper Mint	1/3 oz

Add all the ingredients into a cocktail shaker with 2-3 pieces of ice and give it a long and vigorous shake, pour into a cocktail glass.

Gloom Cocktail

Grenadine	1 dash
Absinthe	1 dash
Gordon Dry Gin	2/3 oz
Italian Vermouth	1/3 oz

Add all the ingredients into a cocktail shaker with 2-3 pieces of ice and shake well, pour into a cocktail glass. Garnish with some lemon peel.

Manhattan Cocktail

Angostura Bitter	1 dash
Curacao	2-3 dash
Whisky	1/2 oz
Italian Vermouth	1/2 oz
Absinthe	1 dash

Add all the ingredients into a mixing glass half-filled with crushed ice and stir well, strain into a cocktail glass. Garnish with a maraschino cherry and some lemon peel.

Martini Cocktail (American style)

Curacao............................1 dash
Maraschino......................1-2 dash
Old Tom Gin.................1/2 oz
French Vermouth..........1/2 oz

Add all the ingredients into a mixing glass half-filled with crushed ice and stir well, strain into a cocktail glass. Garnish with a maraschino cherry and some lemon peel.

Martini Cocktail (English style)

Orange Syrup ....1 dash
Angostura Bitter............1 dash
Plymouth Gin................1/2 oz
French Vermouth..........1/2 oz

Add all the ingredients into a mixing glass half-filled with crushed ice and stir well, strain into a cocktail glass. Garnish with an olive and some lemon peel.

Martini Cocktail

Orange Bitter.................1 dash
Martini & Rossi Vermouth....1/3oz
Gordon Dry Gin...........2/3 oz

Add all the ingredients into a mixing glass half-filled with crushed ice and stir well, strain into a cocktail glass. Garnish with some lemon peel.

Margaret Cocktail

Orange Bitter	1 dash
Maraschino	1 dash
Italian Vermouth	1/3 oz
Tom Gin	2/3 oz

Add all the ingredients into a cocktail shaker with 2-3 pieces of ice and shake well, pour into a cocktail glass.

Mayfair Cocktail

Apricot Syrup	1-2 dash
Clove Syrup	small amount
Orange Juice	1/2 oz
Dry Gin	1/2 oz

Add all the ingredients into a cocktail shaker with 2-3 pieces of ice and shake well, pour into a cocktail glass.

Fairbank Cocktail

Noyau Rose	1 dash
Orange Bitter	1 dash
Gin	1/2 oz
French Vermouth	1/2 oz

Add all the ingredients into a mixing glass half-filled with crushed ice and stir well, strain into a cocktail glass. Garnish with some orange peel.

Fernet Cocktail

          Angostura Bitter............1 dash
          Gomme Syrup...............2 dash
          Fernet Branca ....2/4 oz
          Brandy............................1/4 oz
          Whisky ....1/4 oz

Add all the ingredients into a mixing glass half-filled
with crushed ice and stir well, strain into a cocktail
glass. Garnish with some lemon peel.

Froupe Cocktail

          Benedictine ....1/2 tsp
          Italian Vermouth...........1/2 oz
          Brandy............................1/2 oz

Add all the ingredients into a mixing glass half-filled
with crushed ice and stir well, strain into a cocktail
glass. Garnish with a maraschino cherry and some
lemon peel.

Frankton Cocktail

          Angostura Bitter............2 dash
          White Port.....................1 oz
          Brandy............................small amount

Add all the ingredients into a mixing glass half-filled
with crushed ice and stir well, strain into a cocktail
glass.

Fruit Cocktail

Orange Bitter.................3 dash
Picon............... ....1/2 oz
French Vermouth..........1/2 oz

Add all the ingredients into a mixing glass half-filled with crushed ice and stir well, strain into a cocktail glass.

Ford Cocktail

Dom................................1/2 tsp
Orange Bitter.................2 dash
Tom Gin.... ....1/3 oz
French Vermouth..........2/3 oz

Add all the ingredients into a mixing glass half-filled with crushed ice and stir well, strain into a cocktail glass.

Princess Mary Cocktail

Dry Gin ....1/3 oz
Crème de Cacao ....1/3 oz
Milk.................................1/3 oz

Add all the ingredients into a cocktail shaker with 2-3 pieces of ice and shake well, pour into a cocktail glass.

Princeton Cocktail

      Orange Bitter.................3 dash
      Old Tom Gin.................1 oz

Add both of the ingredients into a cocktail shaker with 2-3 pieces of ice and shake well. Pour into a cocktail glass and add small pour of port wine.

Blackthorn Cocktail

      This cocktail is probably the oldest and the origin of cocktail.
      Orange Bitter.................1 dash
      Angostura Bitter............1 dash
      Sloe Gin.........................1/3 oz
      French Vermouth..........1/3 oz
      Italian Vermouth...........1/3 oz

Add all the ingredients into a mixing glass half-filled with crushed ice and stir well, strain into a cocktail glass. Garnish with some lemon peel.

Bloodhound Cocktail

      Strawberries ....2, crushed
      Maraschino.....................small amount
      Dry Gin..........................1/3 oz
      Italian Vermouth...........1/3 oz
      French Vermouth..........1/3 oz

Add all the ingredients into a cocktail shaker with 2-3 pieces of ice and shake well, pour into a cocktail glass.

$\mathcal{B}$lenton Cocktail

        Angostura Bitter.............1 dash
        Plymouth Gin. ....1/2 oz
        French Vermouth..........1/2 oz

Add all the ingredients into a mixing glass half-filled with crushed ice and stir well, strain into a cocktail glass. Garnish with some lemon peel.

$\mathcal{B}$ronx Cocktail

        Orange Juice. ....1/6 orange
        Dry Gin.......................1/3 oz
        French Vermouth..........1/3 oz
        Italian Vermouth...........1/3 oz

Add all the ingredients into a cocktail shaker with 2-3 pieces of ice and shake well. Pour into a cocktail glass and drop 1 dash of orange bitter.

$\mathcal{B}$razil Cocktail

        Orange Bitter.................1 dash
        Syrup........... ....2 dash
        Absinthe..... ....2 dash
        Dry Sherry _...................1/2 oz
        French Vermouth..........1/2 oz

Add all the ingredients into a mixing glass half-filled with crushed ice and stir well, strain into a cocktail glass. Garnish with some lemon peel.

Brandy Cocktail

Angostura Bitter	1 dash
Curacao	2 dash
Brandy	1 oz

Add all the ingredients into a mixing glass half-filled with crushed ice and stir well, strain into a cocktail glass. Garnish with an olive and some lemon peel.

Coronation Cocktail

Pepper Mint	1 dash
Peach Bitter	1 dash
Curacao	2 dash
Brandy	1 oz

Add all the ingredients into a mixing glass half-filled with crushed ice and stir well, strain into a cocktail glass. Garnish with some lemon peel.

Cornwall Cocktail

Seville Orange Bitter	1/3 oz
Gordon Dry Gin	1/3 oz

Add both of the ingredients into a mixing glass half-filled with crushed ice and stir well, strain into a cocktail glass. Garnish with some lemon peel.

Cooperstown Cocktail (Shake)

                Orange Bitter..................1 dash
                Martini & Rossi Vermouth....1/3 oz
                Gordon Dry Gin...........2/3 oz
                Mint................. ....2 leaves

Add all the ingredients into a cocktail shaker with
2-3 pieces of ice and shake well, pour into a cocktail
glass. Garnish with some lemon peel.

Yellow Cocktail

                Absinthe.........................1/3 oz
                Yellow Chartreuse.........1/3 oz
                Apricot Brandy..............1/3 oz

Add all the ingredients into a cocktail shaker with 2-3
pieces of ice and shake well, pour into a cocktail glass.

Yellow Rattle Cocktail

                Orange Bitter.................1 dash
                Martini & Rossi Vermouth   1/3 oz
                Gordon Dry Gin...........2/3 oz
                Mint................................2 leaves
                Onion (chopped) ....small amount

Add all the ingredients into a cocktail shaker with
2-3 pieces of ice and shake well, pour into a cocktail
glass. Garnish with some lemon peel.

HPW Cocktail

Gin .... 1/3 oz
Italian Vermouth .... 2/3 oz
Orange .... small piece

Add all the ingredients into a cocktail shaker with 2-3 pieces of ice and shake well, pour into a cocktail glass.

HS Cocktail

Orange Bitter .... 3 dash
Gomme Syrup .... 1 dash
Mandarin .... 2 dash
Gin .... 1/2 oz
French Vermouth .... 1/2 oz

Add all the ingredients into a mixing glass half-filled with crushed ice and stir well, strain into a cocktail glass. Garnish with some lemon peel.

XYZ Cocktail

Lemon Juice .... 1 lemon
Dry Gin .... 1/3 oz
French Vermouth .... 1/3 oz
Italian Vermouth .... 1/3 oz

Add all the ingredients into a cocktail shaker with 2-3 pieces of ice and shake well. Pour into a cocktail glass and add some plain syrup or gomme syrup.

Yale Cocktail

Orange Bitter	3 dash
Angostura Bitter	2 dash
Lemon Peel	1 piece
Old Tom Gin	1 oz

Add all the ingredients into a mixing glass half-filled with crushed ice and stir well, add some soda water and pour into a wine glass or champagne glass.

Dubonnet Cocktail

Orange Bitter	1 dash
Angostura Bitter	1 dash
Dubonnet	1/3 oz
Sherry	1/3 oz
French Vermouth	1/3 oz

Add all the ingredients into a cocktail shaker with 2-3 pieces of ice and shake well, pour into a cocktail glass. Garnish with some orange peel.

Diplomat Cocktail

Maraschino	1 dash
French Vermouth	2/3 oz
Italian Vermouth	1/3 oz

Add all the ingredients into a mixing glass half-filled with crushed ice and stir well, strain into a cocktail glass. Garnish with a maraschino cherry and some lemon peel.

Deep Sea Cocktail

Orange Bitter.................1 dash
Absinthe ....1 dash
Old Tom Gin.................1/2 oz
French Vermouth..........1/2 oz

Add all the ingredients into a cocktail shaker with 2-3 pieces of ice and shake well, pour into a cocktail glass. Garnish with an olive and some lemon peel.

Devil Cocktail

Brandy.............................1/2 oz
Crème de Mint or Pepper Mint...1/2 oz

Add both of the ingredients into a cocktail shaker with 2-3 pieces of ice and shake well. Pour into a cocktail glass and add pinch of pepper.

Death Bomb Cocktail

Grenadine......................1/2 tsp
Lemon Juice...................1/2 tsp
Apple Jack Brandy ....1/2 oz
Brandy............................1/2 oz

Add all of the ingredients into a cocktail shaker with 2-3 pieces of ice and shake well, pour into a cocktail glass.

Derby Cocktail

Angostura Bitter	1 dash
Curacao	1 dash
Pineapple Syrup	1 dash
Brandy	1 oz
Champagne	small pour

Add all the ingredients into a mixing glass half-filled with crushed ice and stir quietly, strain into a cocktail glass. Garnish with a maraschino cherry and some lemon peel.

Diablo Cocktail

Angostura Bitter	1 dash
Orange Curacao	2 dash
Brandy	1/2 oz
French Vermouth	1/2 oz

Add all the ingredients into a mixing glass half-filled with crushed ice and stir well, strain into a cocktail glass. Garnish with a maraschino cherry and some lemon peel.

Apricot Cocktail

Angostura Bitter	2 dash
French Vermouth	small pour
Apricot Brandy	1 oz

Add all of the ingredients into a cocktail shaker with 2-3 pieces of ice and shake well, pour into a cocktail glass.

Applejack Cocktail

Angostura Bitter............1 dash
Gomme Syrup or Curacao.....2 dash
Apple Jack Brandy ....1 oz
Sherry.............................small pour

Add all the ingredients into a mixing glass half-filled with crushed ice and stir well, strain into a cocktail glass. Garnish with an olive and some lemon peel.

RAC Cocktail

Dry Gin..........................2/4 oz
French Vermouth..........1/4 oz
Italian Vermouth...........1/4 oz
Grenadine.......................1 dash
Orange Bitter.................1 dash

Add all the ingredients into a mixing glass half-filled with crushed ice and stir well, strain into a cocktail glass. Garnish with a maraschino cherry and some lemon peel.

Irish Cocktail

Gomme Syrup...............1 dash
Angostura Bitter............1 dash
Irish Whisky...................1 oz

Add all of the ingredients into a cocktail shaker with 2-3 pieces of ice and shake well, pour into a cocktail glass. Garnish with some lemon peel.

Amour Cocktail

Angostura Bitter	2 dash
Sherry	½ oz
Italian Vermouth	½ oz

Add all the ingredients into a mixing glass half-filled with crushed ice and stir well, strain into a cocktail glass. Garnish with a maraschino cherry and some lemon peel.

Angler's Cocktail

Angostura Bitter	1 dash
Orange Bitter	1 dash
Gomme syrup	4 dash
Gin	1 oz

Add all the ingredients into a mixing glass half-filled with crushed ice and stir well, strain into a cocktail glass. Garnish with some lemon peel.

Absinthe Cocktail

Angostura Bitter	1 dash
Plain Syrup or Anisette	2 dash
Absinthe	½ oz
Siphon water	½ oz

Add all of the ingredients into a cocktail shaker with 2-3 pieces of ice and shake well, pour into a cocktail glass. Garnish with some lemon peel.

Sidecar Cocktail

Lemon Juice .... 1/3 oz
Cointreau .... 1/3 oz
Brandy .... 1/3 oz

Add all of the ingredients into a cocktail shaker with 2-3 pieces of ice and shake well, pour into a cocktail glass.

Sazerac Cocktail

Sugar cube 1
Angostura bitter .... 1 dash
Whisky .... 1 oz

Add all of the ingredients into a cocktail shaker with 2-3 pieces of ice and shake well, pour into a cocktail glass. Garnish with some lemon peel and add few drops of absinthe.

Cider Cocktail

Sugar cube 1
Angostura bitter .... 2 dash

Add both of the ingredients into a cider glass, add some lemon peel, top up with chilled Mitsuya cider.

St. Martin Cocktail

Gin .... ½ oz
Italian vermouth .... ½ oz
Yellow chartreuse .... ½ tsp

Add all of the ingredients into a cocktail shaker with 2-3 pieces of ice and shake well, pour into a cocktail glass. Garnish with some lemon peel.

Sensation Cocktail

Maraschino	2 dash
Mint	2 leaves
Lime juice	1/3 oz
Dry gin	2/3 oz

Add all of the ingredients into a cocktail shaker with 2-3 pieces of ice and shake well, pour into a cocktail glass.

Sun prince Cocktail

Angostura bitter	3 dash
Curacao	3 dash
Dry Whisky	½ oz
Golden Sherry	½ oz

Add all of the ingredients into a cocktail shaker with 2-3 pieces of ice and shake well, pour into a cocktail glass.

Sunshine Cocktail

Orange bitter	1 dash
Old Tom Gin	1/3 oz
French Vermouth	1/3 oz
Italian Vermouth	1/3 oz

Add all the ingredients into a mixing glass half-filled with crushed ice and stir well, strain into a cocktail glass. Garnish with some lemon peel.

Cuban Cocktail

Orange bitter .... 2 dash
Maraschino .... 1 dash
French Vermouth .... 1/3 oz
Dry Gin .... 1/3 oz

Add all the ingredients into a mixing glass half-filled with crushed ice and stir well, strain into a cocktail glass. Garnish with a maraschino cherry and some lemon peel.

Medium Martini Cocktail

Gordon Dry Gin .... 4/6 oz
Martini & Rossi Vermouth   1/6 oz
French Vermouth .... 1/6 oz

Add all the ingredients into a mixing glass half-filled with crushed ice and stir well, strain into a cocktail glass. Garnish with some lemon peel.

Meehoulong Cocktail

Orange bitter .... 1 dash
Sloe Gin .... 4/6 oz
French Vermouth .... 1/6 oz
Italian Vermouth .... 1/6 oz

Add all the ingredients into a mixing glass half-filled with crushed ice and stir well, strain into a cocktail glass. Garnish with some lemon peel.

Metropole Cocktail

Gomme syrup	2 dash
Angostura bitter	2 dash
Orange bitter	2 dash
Brandy	½ oz
French Vermouth	½ oz

Add all of the ingredients into a cocktail shaker with 2-3 pieces of ice and shake well, pour into a cocktail glass. Garnish with a piece of pineapple and a maraschino cherry.

Mikado Cocktail (Japanese Cocktail)

Angostura bitter	1 dash
Noyau	1 dash
Orgeat	1 dash
Curacao	1 dash
Brandy	1 oz

Add all the ingredients into a mixing glass half-filled with crushed ice and stir well, strain into a cocktail glass. Garnish with some lemon peel.

Millionaire Cocktail

Egg white	1 Egg
Curacao	1 dash
Grenadine	1/3 oz
Whisky	2/3 oz

Add all of the ingredients into a cocktail shaker with 2-3 pieces of ice and shake well. Pour into a cocktail glass and add a small pour of absinthe.

Chicago Cocktail

Angostura bitter............ 1 dash
French Vermouth.......... ½ oz
Plymouth Gin................. ½ oz
Champagne .... small pour

Add all the ingredients into a mixing glass half-filled with crushed ice and stir quietly, strain into a cocktail glass. Garnish with some lemon peel.

Silver Cocktail

Maraschino..................... 1-2 dash
Orange bitter .... 2 dash
Gin .... ½ oz
French Vermouth.......... ½ oz

Add all the ingredients into a mixing glass half-filled with crushed ice and stir well, strain into a cocktail glass. Garnish with some lemon peel.

Silver Streak Cocktail

Kummel........................... ½ oz
Dry Gin .... ½ oz

Add all of the ingredients into a cocktail shaker with 2-3 pieces of ice and shake well, pour into a cocktail glass.

Champagne Cocktail

Sugar .... 1 tsp
Angostura bitter .... 2 dash

Add both of the ingredients into a champagne glass with some ice cubes, top up with chilled champagne and stir quietly. Garnish with some lemon peel.

Shamrock Cocktail

Curacao .... 3 dash
Ginger Ale .... small pour
Whisky ....._..................... 1 oz

Add all of the ingredients into a cocktail shaker with 2-3 pieces of ice and shake well, pour into a cocktail glass. Garnish with some lemon peel.

Gibson Cocktail

Orange bitter .... 1 dash
Martini & Rossi Vermouth ... 1/3 oz
Gordon Dry Gin .... 2/3 oz
Chopped onion .... small amount

Add all the ingredients into a mixing glass half-filled with crushed ice and stir well, strain into a cocktail glass. Garnish with some lemon peel.

Jack Rose Cocktail

Lime juice	1/3 oz
Raspberry syrup	small pour
Apple Jack Brandy	2/3 oz

Add all of the ingredients into a cocktail shaker with 2-3 pieces of ice and shake well, pour into a cocktail glass.

Jamaican Rum Cocktail

Orange bitter	1 dash
Gomme syrup	2 dash
Jamaican Rum	1 oz

Add all the ingredients into a mixing glass half-filled with crushed ice and stir well, strain into a cocktail glass. Garnish with some lemon peel.

Ping-pong Cocktail

Angostura bitter	1 dash
Curacao	1-2 dash
Sloe Gin	½ oz
Italian Vermouth	½ oz
Absinthe	1 dash

Add all the ingredients into a mixing glass half-filled with crushed ice and stir well, strain into a cocktail glass. Garnish with a maraschino cherry and some lemon peel.

Puritan Cocktail

Gomme syrup .... 1 dash
Orange bitter .... 2 dash
Chartreuse .... small pour
French Vermouth .... ½ oz
Gin .... ½ oz

Add all of the ingredients into a cocktail shaker with
2-3 pieces of ice and shake well, pour into a cocktail
glass. Garnish with some lemon peel.

Bijou Cocktail

Orange bitter .... 1 dash
Plymouth Gin .... 1/3 oz
Italian Vermouth .... 1/3 oz
Green Chartreuse .... 1/3 oz

Add all the ingredients into a mixing glass half-filled
with crushed ice and stir well, strain into a cocktail
glass. Garnish with an olive or a maraschino cherry
and some lemon peel.

Morning Cocktail

Curacao .... 1 dash
Maraschino .... 1 dash
Orange bitter .... 1 dash
Absinthe .... 1 dash
Brandy .... ½ oz
French Vermouth .... ½ oz

Add all the ingredients into a mixing glass half-filled
with crushed ice and stir well, strain into a cocktail glass.
Garnish with a maraschino cherry and some lemon peel.

Monkey Gland Cocktail

Absinthe	1 tsp
Grenadine	1 tsp
Dry Gin	½ oz
Orange juice	½ oz

Add all of the ingredients into a cocktail shaker with 2-3 pieces of ice and shake well, pour into a cocktail glass.

Sherry Cocktail

Golden Sherry	1 oz
Curacao	3 dash

Add both of the ingredients into a mixing glass half-filled with crushed ice and stir well, strain into a cocktail glass. Garnish with some orange peel.

Stinger Cocktail

Pepper mint	1/3 oz
Old Brandy	2/3 oz

Add all of the ingredients into a cocktail shaker with 2-3 pieces of ice and shake well, pour into a cocktail glass.

The Star Cocktail

Orange bitter	2 dash
Orange Curacao	1 dash
French Vermouth	½ oz
Apple Jack Brandy	½ oz

Add both of the ingredients into a mixing glass half-filled with crushed ice and stir well, strain into a cocktail glass. Garnish with an olive and some orange peel.

Spanish Cocktail

Angostura bitter............2 dash
Italian Vermouth...........1 oz

Add all of the ingredients into a cocktail shaker with 2-3 pieces of ice and shake well. Rub the inside of a cocktail glass with lemon peel, pour the cocktail into the glass and garnish with some lemon peel.

Sterling Cocktail

Curacao......... ....¼ oz
Maraschino.....................¼ oz
Dom................................¼ oz
Absinthe...... ....¼ oz
Egg yolk ....1 egg

Add all the ingredients into a large cocktail glass with some salt and stir well.

Sloe Gin Cocktail

Orange bitter.................1 dash
Crème de Cacao............3 dash
Booth's Gin....................1 oz

Add all of the ingredients into a cocktail shaker with 2-3 pieces of ice and shake well, pour into a cocktail glass. Garnish with some lemon peel.

Los Cocktail

Strawberries .... 3-4, crushed
Pineapple .... small piece
Lemon juice .... ½ lemon
Orange juice .... orange

Add all of the ingredients into a cocktail shaker with 2-3 pieces of ice and shake well, pour into a cocktail glass.

Oyster Cocktail

Tomato Ketchup .... 3 tsp
Lemon juice .... ¼ lemon
Salt and pepper .... a pinch
Worcestershire Sauce .... 1 tsp
Oyster 5-6

Mix all the ingredients and place into a sherbet glass. Place the glass on the crushed ice and serve.

Lobster Cocktail
Crab Cocktail

Use the same method with Oyster Cocktail, replace oyster with boiled lobster or boiled crab.

Pacific Cocktail

Lemon Juice	1 lemon
Orange juice	1 orange
Plain syrup	small pour
Mint	2 leaves
Egg white	½ egg

Add all of the ingredients into a cocktail shaker with 2-3 pieces of ice and shake well, pour into a wine glass.

Tomato Cocktail

Put a ripe tomato into boiling water for about 1 minute, take the tomato out of water, peel and slice it. Place the tomato into a sherbet glass following with some orange peel, ½ tsp of Mayonnaise, a dash of vinegar and olive oil. Garnish with chopped parsley and place the glass on crushed ice to serve.

Wedge Cocktail

Worcestershire Sauce	small amount
Tomato Ketchup	2 tsp
Mustard	small amount
Salt and pepper	a pinch
Lemon juice	¼ lemon
Grilled chicken	small pieces
Matsutake mushroom	small pieces

Mix all the ingredients and place into a champagne glass, Garnish with nutmeg powder and serve.

Vegetable Cocktail

Mix vegetable salad and some white sauce, place it into a sherbet glass and garnish with some herbs. (nutmeg, yuzu, parsley etc) Place the glass on the crushed ice to serve.

Florida Cocktail

Lemon juice	1 lemon
Orange juice	½ lemon
Angostura bitter	3 dash
Gomme syrup	1-2 dash

Add all of the ingredients into a cocktail shaker with 2-3 pieces of ice and shake well, pour into a cocktail glass.

Jersey Cocktail

Gomme syrup	3 dash
Angostura bitter	1-2 dash
Mitsuya cider	half of bottle

Add all the ingredients into a mixing glass half-filled with crushed ice, stir well and strain into a wine glass. Garnish with a maraschino cherry and some lemon peel.

Punch

Imperial Punch

Sugar	1 tsp
Claret	5 oz
Whisky	½ oz

Add all the ingredients into a punch glass with 2-3 pieces of ice and stir well. Add some nutmeg powder and seasonal fruit, top up with soda water.

Roman Punch

Navel juice	½ navel
Lemon juice	½ lemon
Sugar	1 tsp
Rum	1 oz
Brandy	1 oz

Add all the ingredients into a punch glass with 2-3 pieces of ice and stir well. Add some fruit pieces, top up with soda water.

Bangkok Cocktail

Sugar	1 tsp
Lemon juice	½ lemon
Whisky	1 oz
Rum	1 oz

Add all the ingredients into a punch glass with 2-3 pieces of ice and stir well. Add some seasonal fruit, top up with soda water.

Hot Rum Punch

Sugar	1 tsp
Lemon juice	¼ lemon
Rum	2 oz

Ad all the ingredients into a punch glass, top up with hot water and add some fruit pieces.

Dragon Punch (10 serve)

Brandy	2 oz
Sherry	2 oz
Stout	1 small bottle
Lager beer	1 small bottle
Champagne	1 bottle

Add all the ingredients into a large jug with 1-2 pieces of ice and stir, add some sugar and lemon peel to see your taste, serve in champagne glass.

Chocolate Punch

Sugar	1 tsp
Egg	1
Lemon juice	½ lemon
Port wine	2 oz
Brandy	1 oz

Add all of the ingredients into a cocktail shaker half-filled with crushed ice, shake well, pour into a punch glass and top up with soda water.

Tip Top Punch

Orange	1 piece
Pineapple	1 piece
Brandy	1 oz

Add all the ingredients into a punch glass with 2-3 pieces of ice and stir well, top up with champagne.

Orange Punch

Sugar	1 tsp
Lemon juice	½ lemon
Orange juice	½ orange
Orange Brandy	2 oz

Add all the ingredients into a punch glass with 2-3 pieces of ice and stir well. Add some seasonal fruit, top up with soda water.

National Punch

Sugar	1 tsp
Lemon juice	½ lemon
Brandy	1 oz
Dom	1 oz

Add all of the ingredients into a cocktail shaker half-filled with crushed ice, shake well, pour into a wine glass and add dash of Jamaican Rum.

Rum Punch

Sugar	1 tsp
Lemon juice	¼ lemon
Rum	2 oz

Ad all the ingredients into a punch glass with 2-3 pieces of ice and stir well, top up with soda water.

West Indian Punch

Sugar	1 tsp
Lemon juice	½ lemon
Brandy	½ oz
Madeira	2 oz

Add all of the ingredients into a cocktail shaker half-filled with ice, shake well, pour into a wine glass and top with some strawberries and grapes.

Whisky Punch

Sugar	1 tsp
Lemon juice	½ lemon
Whisky	2 oz

Add all the ingredients into a mixing glass half-filled with ice and stir well, pour into a wine glass.

Claret Punch

Sugar	1 tsp
Lemon juice	¼ lemon
Claret	4 oz

Add all the ingredients into a punch glass with 2 oz of water and a piece of ice. Serve with spoon.

Manhattan Punch

Sugar	½ tsp
Lemon juice	½ lemon
Angostura bitter	2 dashes
Whisky	1 oz
Vermouth	1 oz

Add all of the ingredients into a cocktail shaker half-filled with ice, shake well, pour into a punch glass and top up with soda water.

Planter Punch

            Sugar syrup .... 1 tsp
            Lime juice .... 1 lime
            Bacardi .... 4 oz

Add all of the ingredients into a cocktail shaker half-
filled with ice, shake well, pour into a water glass and
top with a sprinkle of nutmeg powder.

Brandy Punch

            Sugar .... 1 tsp
            Lemon juice .... ½ lemon
            Brandy .... 2 oz

Add all of the ingredients into a cocktail shaker half-
filled with ice, shake well, pour into a punch glass and
top up with soda water.

Brandy Milk Punch

            Sugar .... ½ tsp
            Brandy .... 2 oz

Add all of the ingredients into a cocktail shaker half-
filled with ice, shake well, pour into a punch glass.
Top up with milk and a sprinkle of nutmeg powder.

Curacao Punch

Sugar	½ tsp
Lemon juice	½ lemon
Curacao	1 oz
Brandy	1 oz

Add all of the ingredients into a cocktail shaker half-filled with ice, shake well, pour into a punch glass. Top up with small pour of Jamaica Rum and soda water.

Milk Punch

Sugar syrup	1 tsp
Rum	1 oz
Brandy	2 oz
Milk	180 ml

Add all of the ingredients into a cocktail shaker half-filled with ice, shake well, pour into a punch glass and top with a sprinkle of nutmeg powder.

Champagne Punch

Sugar syrup	1 tsp
Lemon juice	½ lemon
Curacao	1 tsp

Add all of the ingredients into a cocktail shaker half-filled with ice, shake well, pour into a wine glass and top up with chilled champagne.

Gin Punch

Egg	1
Sugar	1 tsp
Dry Gin	1 oz

Add all the ingredients into a punch glass with 2-3 pieces of ice and stir well. Top up with soda water and a sprinkle of nutmeg powder.

Japanese Punch

Sugar	½ tsp
Lemon juice	½ lemon
Alcohol	1 oz (unclear what kind)
Brandy	1 oz

Add all the ingredients into a punch glass and top up with warm Sake.

Rickys

Royal Ricky

Lemon juice	¼ lemon
Lime juice	½ lime
Raspberry syrup	1 tsp
French Vermouth	2 oz
Gin	1 oz

Add all the ingredients into a water glass and stir well, top up with soda water and some seasonal fruits.

Canadian Ricky

Lemon juice	½ lemon
Canadian whisky	2 oz

Add both of the ingredients into a water glass with 2-3 pieces of ice and top up with soda water. Serve with a spoon.

Brandy Ricky

Lemon juice	½ lemon
Sugar syrup	1 tsp
Brandy	2 oz

Add all the ingredients into a water glass with 2-3 pieces of ice and top up with soda water. Serve with a spoon.

Sloe Gin Ricky

Lime juice .... ½ lime
Sloe Gin .... 3 oz

Add both of the ingredients into a water glass with
2-3 pieces of ice and top up with soda water. Serve
with a spoon.

$\mathcal{C}$ups

$\mathcal{I}$ndian cup

Sugar	1 tsp
Lemon peel	1 piece
Claret	3 oz
Curacao	½ oz
Madeira wine	½ oz

Add all the ingredients into a punch glass with some cucumber and top up with soda water.

$\mathcal{R}$oyal Cup

Sugar	1 tsp
Lemon juice	1 lemon
Brandy	2 oz
Curacao	1 oz
Maraschino	small pour
Pineapple	4-5 pieces
Claret	1 bottle
Soda water	1 bottle
Champagne	1 bottle

Add all the ingredients into a large jug with some ice and stir softly. Serve in a champagne glass.

Balaklava Cup

Lemon juice	1 lemon
Sugar	1 tsp
Claret	1 bottle
Champagne	1 bottle

Ad all the ingredients into a jug with some ice and stir softly. Serve in a champagne glass.

Badminton Cup

Sherry	1 oz
Maraschino	½ oz
Sugar	small amount
Claret	1 oz
Cucumber peel	small piece

Add all the ingredients into a water glass and stir well, top with some chopped parsley.

Lincoln Club Cup (10 serves)

Lemon juice	1 lemon
Orange juice	½ orange
Brandy	2 oz
Sherry	2 oz
Port wine	2 oz
Champagne	1 bottle
Soda water	1 bottle

Add all the ingredients into a large jug with some ice and stir softly. Serve in a champagne glass.

Orange Cup

Orange juice	½ orange
Lemon juice	½ lemon
Gomme syrup	small pour
Soda water	1 bottle

Add all the ingredients into a jug with some ice and stir softly. Serve in a water glass.

Line Wine Cup

Lemon	1 piece
Orange	1 piece
Curacao	1 oz
Brandy	1 oz
Line wine	1 bottle
Soda water	1 bottle

Add all the ingredients into a large jug with some ice and stir softly, add 2-3 leaves of mint and serve in a champagne glass.

Claret Cup

Lemon juice	½ lemon
Curacao	1 oz
Brandy	2 oz
Claret	1 bottle
Soda water	1 bottle

Add all the ingredients into a large jug with some ice and stir softly, add some nutmeg powder and serve in a champagne glass.

Madeira Cup (5-6 serves)

Lemon juice	1 lemon
Mandarinet	2 oz
Dry Madeira Wine	1 bottle
Soda water	1 bottle

Add all the ingredients into a large jug with some ice and stir softly. Serve in a water glass.

Mamola Cup

Sugar	1 tsp
Lemon juice	½ lemon
Maraschino	½ oz
Rum	½ oz
Brandy	½ oz
Syrup	2 oz

Add all the ingredients into a punch glass with some ice and stir well, top up with champagne. Garnish with some mint.

Cambridge Claret Cup (10 serves)

Sugar	1 tsp
Lemon juice	lemon
Brandy	1 oz
Curacao	1 oz
Claret	540 ml
Sherry	540 ml
Soda water	540 ml

Add all the ingredients into a large jug with some ice and stir softly. Top with some cucumber peel and some fruits. Serve in a water glass.

Cider Cup

Sugar	small amount
Sherry	4 oz
Curacao	2 oz
Brandy	2 oz

Add all the ingredients into a water glass and top up with Mitsuya Cider. Garnish with some lemon peel.

Champagne Cup (10 serves)

Abricotine	1 oz
Curacao	1 oz
Brandy	2 oz
Champagne	1 bottle
Soda water	1 bottle

Add all the ingredients into a large jug with some ice and stir softly. Add some herbs such as nutmeg or mint to finish, serve in a champagne glass.

Lemonades

Orange Squash

Orange juice	½ orange
Sugar	½ tsp

Add both of the ingredients into a bar glass with 2-3 pieces of ice and top up with soda water. Garnish with some lemon peel and serve with a straw.

Lemon Squash

Use the same method as with the Orange Squash, replace orange with lemon.

Lemonade claret

Lemon juice	½ lemon
Sugar	1 tsp
Claret	2 oz

Add all the ingredients into a bar glass and top up with soda water. Serve with a straw.

Lemonade

Lemon juice	¼ lemon
Sugar	1 tsp

Add both of the ingredients into a bar glass and top up with hot water.

Fruit Lemonade

Lemon juice....	2 oz
Orange juice...................	2 oz
Grenadine.......................	1-2 dashes
Mint..............	2-3 leaves

Add all the ingredients into a cocktail shaker and shake well, pour into a bar glass and top up with soda water.

American Lemonade

Lemon juice	½ lemon
Sugar	1 tsp
Port wine.......................	2 oz

Add all the ingredients into a bar glass and top up with soda water. Serve with a straw.

Coolers

Imperial Cooler

Lemon juice	½ lemon
Claret	1 oz
Cocoa or chocolate	small amount

Add all the ingredients into a water glass and stir well, top up with soda water.

Rocky Mountain Cooler

Egg yolk	1 egg
Sugar syrup	2-3 dashes
Lemon juice	1 lemon

Add all the ingredients into a cocktail shaker with 2-3 pieces of ice and give it a long vigorous shake, pour into a water glass, top up with Mitsuya cider and a sprinkle of nutmeg powder.

Tod's Cooler

Lemon juice	½ lemon
Dry Gin	2 oz
Cassis de Dijon	1 oz

Add all the ingredients into a water glass with 2-3 pieces of ice and stir well, top up with soda water.

Cablegram Cooler

        Lemon juice .... ½ lemon
        Whisky............ .... 3 oz
        Gomme syrup .... small amount

Add all the ingredients into a water glass with 2-3
pieces of ice and stir well, top up with ginger ale.

Brunswick Cooler

        Lemon juice .. .. 1 lemon
        Sugar syrup .... 1 tsp

Add all the ingredients into a water glass with 2-3
pieces of ice and top up with ginger ale.

Bulldog Cooler

        Lemon juice .... ½ lemon
        Dry Gin........ .... 3 oz
        Gomme syrup .... small amount

Add all the ingredients into a water glass with 2-3
pieces of ice and stir well, top up with ginger ale.

Saratoga Cooler

        Lime juice......................... 1 lime
        Sugar syrup .... 1 tsp

Add all the ingredients into a water glass with 2-3
pieces of ice and top up with ginger ale.

Zenith Cooler

Pineapple	1 piece
Sugar syrup	1 tsp
Dry Gin	4 oz

Add all the ingredients into a water glass with 2-3 pieces of ice and stir, top up with soda water.

Crustas

Whisky Crusta

Gomme syrup	3 dashes
Maraschino	3 dashes
Angostura bitter	2 dashes
Lemon juice	¼ lemon
Whisky	1 oz

Add all the ingredients into a cocktail shaker with 2-3 pieces of ice and shake well, pour into a water glass and garnish with some orange peel.

Gin Crusta

Gomme syrup	3 dashes
Maraschino	3 dashes
Angostura bitter	2 dashes
Lemon juice	¼ lemon
Dry Gin	1 oz

Add all the ingredients into a cocktail shaker with 2-3 pieces of ice and shake well, pour into a water glass and garnish with some orange peel.

Fizzes

Royal Fizz

Grenadine	1 tsp
Egg white	1 egg
Orange juice	½ orange
Dry Gin	2 oz

Add all the ingredients into a cocktail shaker half-filled with ice and shake well, pour into a punch glass and top up with soda water.

New Orleans Fizz

Sugar syrup	1 tsp
Lemon juice	½ lemon
Dry Gin	2 oz
Milk	2 oz

Add all the ingredients into a cocktail shaker half-filled with ice and shake well, pour into a punch glass and top up with soda water.

Orange Fizz

Sugar syrup	1 tsp
Orange juice	½ orange
Dry Gin	2 oz

Add all the ingredients into a cocktail shaker half-filled with ice and shake well, pour into a punch glass and top up with soda water.

Soda Fizz

Sugar .... 1 tsp
Lemon juice .... ½ lemon

Add both of the ingredients into a punch glass with
2-3 pieces of ice and top up with soda water. Garnish
with some mint leaves.

Violet Fizz

Sugar syrup .... 1 tsp
Lime juice .... 2 dashes
Dry Gin .... 2 oz
Egg white .... 1 egg

Add all the ingredients into a cocktail shaker half-filled
with ice and shake well, pour into a punch glass and
top up with soda water.

Whisky Fizz

Sugar syrup .... 1 tsp
Lemon juice .... ½ lemon
Whisky .... 2 oz

Add all the ingredients into a cocktail shaker half-filled
with ice and shake well, pour into a punch glass and
top up with soda water.

Cream Fizz

Sugar syrup	1 tsp
Lemon juice	1 lemon
Cream	small amount
Dry Gin	2 oz

Add all the ingredients into a cocktail shaker half-filled with ice and shake well, pour into a punch glass and top up with soda water.

French Fizz

Gomme syrup	4 dashes
Lemon juice	½ lemon
French Vermouth	2 oz

Add all the ingredients into a cocktail shaker half-filled with ice and shake well, pour into a punch glass and top up with soda water.

Brandy Fizz

Use the same method as with the French Fizz, replace French Vermouth with Brandy.

Golden Fizz

Sugar syrup	1 tsp
Egg yolk	1 egg
Lemon juice	1 lemon
Dry Gin	2 oz

Add all the ingredients into a cocktail shaker half-filled with ice and shake well, pour into a punch glass and top up with soda water.

Texas Fizz

Lemon juice .... ½ lemon
Orange juice .... ½ orange
Grenadine .... few dashes
Dry Gin .... 3 oz

Add all the ingredients into a cocktail shaker half-filled with ice and shake well, pour into a punch glass and top up with soda water.

Gin Fizz

Sugar syrup .... 1 tsp
Lemon juice .... 1 lemon
Dry Gin .... 2 oz

Add all the ingredients into a cocktail shaker half-filled with ice and shake well, pour into a punch glass and top up with soda water.

Morning Glory Fizz

Egg white .... 1 egg
Sugar syrup .... few dashes
Lemon juice .... ½ lemon
Absinthe .... 3 dashes
Gin, Brandy or Whisky .... 3 oz

Add all the ingredients into a cocktail shaker half-filled with ice and shake well, pour into a punch glass and top up with soda water.

Flips

Boston Flip

Egg yolk	1 egg
Sugar syrup	few dashes
Madeira	1 oz
Whisky	1 oz

Add all the ingredients into a cocktail shaker half-filled with ice and shake well, pour into a wine glass and top with a sprinkle of nutmeg powder.

Lemon Flip

Egg yolk	1 egg
Sugar syrup	few dashes
Lemon juice	½ lemon

Add all the ingredients into a cocktail shaker half-filled with ice and shake well, pour into a wine glass and top with a sprinkle of nutmeg powder.

Brandy Flip

Egg white	1 egg
Maraschino	few dashes
Brandy	2 oz

Add all the ingredients into a cocktail shaker half-filled with ice and shake well, pour into a wine glass and top with a sprinkle of nutmeg powder.

Golden Flip

Egg yolk	1 egg
Maraschino	1 oz
Yellow Chartreuse	1 oz
Sugar	small amount

Add all the ingredients into a cocktail shaker half-filled with ice and shake well, pour into a wine glass and top with a sprinkle of nutmeg powder.

Champagne Flip

Add an egg yolk into a cocktail shaker half-filled with ice and shake well, add 180ml of champagne and mix, pour into a champagne glass. Top with a sprinkle of sugar and nutmeg powder.

Gin Flip

Egg yolk	1 egg
Sugar syrup	few dashes
Dry Gin	2 oz

Add all the ingredients into a cocktail shaker half-filled with ice and shake well, pour into a wine glass and top with a sprinkle of nutmeg powder.

Sherry Flip

Egg yolk	1 egg
Sugar syrup	few dashes
Dry Bar Sherry	3 oz

Add all the ingredients into a cocktail shaker half-filled with ice and shake well, pour into a wine glass and top with a sprinkle of nutmeg powder.

Claret Flip

Use the same method as with the Sherry Flip, replace Dry Bar Sherry with whisky or claret. Adjust amount depending on percentage of alcohol and flavour desired.

$\mathcal{P}$ousse-cafe
(Five-colour layered cocktail)

$\mathcal{P}$ousse-café (American style)

> Raspberry syrup .... 1 tsp
> Maraschino .... 1/5 of a glass
> Crème de Vanille .... 1/5 of a glass
> Red Curacao .... 1/5 of a glass
> Yellow Chartreuse .... 1/5 of a glass
> Old Brandy .... 1/5 of a glass

Pour all the ingredients into a pousse-café glass softly by following the order of the recipe one after the other to make the layers. Serve with a short straw.

$\mathcal{P}$ousse-café (French style)

> Framboise syrup .... 1/5 of a glass
> Maraschino .... 1/5 of a glass
> Curacao Rocher .... 1/5 of a glass
> Chartreuse Jaune .... 1/5 of a glass
> Champagne .... 1/5 of a glass

Pour all the ingredients into a pousse-café glass softly by following the order of the recipe one after the other to make the layers. Serve with a short straw.

Cobblers

Whisky Cobbler

Gomme syrup ....2 dashes
Maraschino.....................2 dashes
Whisky............................1 oz

Add all the ingredients into a water glass ¾ filled with water and stir, garnish with some seasonal fruits.

Claret cobbler

Sugar ....1 tsp
Claret...............................4 oz

Add both of the ingredients into a water glass ¼ filled with ice and stir, garnish with some seasonal fruits.

Champagne cobbler

Sugar cube......................1
Lemon peel ....small piece

Add both of the ingredients into a champagne glass with a piece of ice and top up with champagne.

Sherry Cobbler

Sugar syrup .... ½ tsp
Curacao........................... ½ tsp
Sherry............. .... 1 oz

Add all the ingredients into a mixing glass half-filled with ice and stir well, pour into a sherbet glass. Garnish with some seasonal fruits and serve with a straw and a spoon.

Eggnog

Boston Eggnog

Egg	1
Sugar syrup	½ tsp
Madeira	3 oz
Brandy	1 oz
Jamaican Rum	1 oz

Add all the ingredients into a cocktail shaker with 2-3 pieces of ice, add some milk and shake well, pour into a punch glass and top with a sprinkle of nutmeg powder.

Chinese Eggnog

Egg	1
Crème de Cacao	1 tsp
Dom	1 tsp
Brandy	2 oz

Add all the ingredients into a cocktail shaker with 2-3 pieces of ice, add some milk and shake well, pour into a punch glass and top with a sprinkle of nutmeg powder.

Plain Eggnog

Egg	1
Sugar syrup	½ tsp
Brandy	3 oz

Add all the ingredients into a cocktail shaker with 2-3 pieces of ice, add some milk and shake well, pour into a punch glass and top with a sprinkle of nutmeg powder.

Replace Brandy with any other desired spirits.

Breakfast Eggnog

Egg	1
Orange Curacao	1 ½ oz
Old Brandy	3 oz

Add all the ingredients into a cocktail shaker with 2-3 pieces of ice, add some milk and shake well, pour into a punch glass and top with a sprinkle of nutmeg powder.

Eggnog

Egg	1
Sugar syrup	½ tsp
Brandy	2 oz
Rum	1 oz

Add all the ingredients into a cocktail shaker with 2-3 pieces of ice, add some milk and shake well, pour into a punch glass and top with a sprinkle of nutmeg powder.

General Harrison Eggnog

Egg	1
Sugar syrup	few dashes
Lemon juice	1 lemon

Add all the ingredients into a cocktail shaker with 2-3 pieces of ice, add some milk and shake well, pour into a punch glass and top with a sprinkle of nutmeg powder.

Cider Eggnog

Add small pour of sugar syrup and an egg into a punch glass half-filled with ice and stir well. Top up with Mitsuya cider and a sprinkle of nutmeg powder.

Daisy

Rum Daisy

Lemon juice .... ½ lemon
Curacao or Yellow Chartreuse.... ½ oz
Rum .... 2 oz

Add all the ingredients into a cocktail shaker with 2-3 pieces of ice, small pour of water and shake well. Pour into a wine glass and top with some seasonal fruits.

Morning Glory Daisy

Egg white 1
Lemon juice .... ½ lemon
Sugar syrup .... 1 tsp
Gin, Whisky or brandy..... 2 oz
Absinthe .... 3 dashes

Add all the ingredients into a cocktail shaker with 2-3 pieces of ice, shake well, pour into a wine glass.

$\mathscr{S}$ours

$\mathscr{W}$hisky Sour

Gomme syrup .... 3 dashes
Lemon juice .... ¼ lemon
Whisky .... 2 oz

Add all the ingredients into a cocktail shaker half-filled with ice, shake well and pour into a wine glass. Top with small pour of soda water and some seasonal fruits.

$\mathscr{G}$in Sour

Use the same method as with the Whisky Sour, replace Whisky with Brandy or Gin.

$\mathscr{E}$gg Sour

Plane Syrup .... small amount
Egg 1
Lemon Juice .... ¼ lemon

Add all the ingredients into a cocktail shaker half-filled with ice, shake well and pour into a wine glass. Top with small pour of soda water and some seasonal fruits.

Champagne Sour

        Sugar .... 1 tsp
        Lemon juice ....._............ small amount

Add both of the ingredients into a champagne glass
with a piece of ice and top up with champagne,
Garnish with some fruits.

Strawberry Sour

        Sugar .... 1 tsp
        Strawberries 5
        Brandy..........._.................. 2 oz

Add all the ingredients into a mixing glass half-filled
with ice and stir well, pour into a water glass and top
up with chilled milk.

Juleps

Pineapple Julep (5-6 serves)

Sparkling Moselle	720 ml
Gomme syrup	1 oz
Maraschino	1 oz
Old Tom Gin	1 oz
Orange Bitter	1 oz
Navel juice	5 navels
Lemon juice	2 lemons
Pineapple	few pieces
Sugar	2 tsp

Add all the ingredients into a large jug with some ice, top up with soda water. Serve in wine glass.

Old George Julep

Sugar	½ tsp
Brandy	2 ½ oz
Apricot Brandy	2 ½ oz
Mint	2-3 leaves

Add all the ingredients into a bar glass with some ice, top up with water and stir well.

Whisky Julep

Sugar ....1 tsp
Mint.............. ....2-3 leaves
Whisky ....2 oz

Add all the ingredients into a cocktail shaker half-filled with ice and give it a strong shake, pour into a wine glass.

Garnish with some fruits.

Gin Julep

Use the same method as with the Whisky Julep, replace Whisky with Brandy or Gin.

Slings

Hot Whisky Sling

Sugar	½ tsp
Whisky	2 oz

Add the both of ingredients into a water glass and top up with hot water. Garnish with some lemon peel and a sprinkle of nutmeg powder.

Hot Brandy Sling

Use the same method as with the Hot Whisky Sling, replace Whisky with Brandy.

Straight Sling

Orange bitter	2 dashes
Angostura bitter	2 dashes
Lemon juice	½ lemon
Dom	½ oz
Brandy	½ oz
Old Tom Gin	2 oz

Add all the ingredients into a cocktail shaker with 2-3 pieces of ice and shake well. Pour into a water glass and top up with soda water.

Others

Royal Smile

Lemon juice .... ½ lemon
Grenadine...... .... 1 tsp
Dry Gin .... 2 oz
Apple Jack Brandy .... 1 oz

Add all the ingredients into a cocktail shaker half-filled with ice and shake well, pour into a wine glass. Top with some cream.

White Lion

Lemon juice .... ½ lemon
Raspberry syrup .... 1 oz
Curacao........................... 1 oz
Rum............ .... 3 oz

Add all the ingredients into a cocktail shaker and shake, pour into a water glass with a piece of ice. Garnish with some seasonal fruits.

Hot Apple Toddy

Apple juice .... 1 apple
Brandy.... .... 3 oz

Place a sugar cube with a dash of hot water into a water glass, add all the ingredients into the glass and stir well. Top up with hot water and a sprinkle of nutmeg powder.

$\mathcal{B}$osom Caresser 1

Gomme syrup	1 tsp
Egg	½ egg
Brandy	2 oz
Milk	180 ml

Add all the ingredients into a mixing glass half-filled with ice and stir well. Strain into a punch glass.

$\mathcal{P}$ort Wine Negus

Sugar cube	1
Port Wine	1 oz

Add both of the ingredients into a water glass, top up with hot water and a sprinkle of nutmeg powder.

$\mathcal{P}$unch A La Romaine (10 serves)

Orange bitter	2 tsp
Lemon juice	2 lemons
Orange juice	2 oranges
Sugar	100 g
Egg	7

Add all the ingredients into a large jug and stir well. Add a bottle of Rum, A bottle of Champagne and stir. Serve in a champagne glass.

Bosom Caresser 2

Egg yolk	1 egg
Madeira	1 oz
Brandy	1 oz
Curacao	1 oz
Grenadine	1 oz

Add all the ingredients into a cocktail glass half-filled with ice and shake well. Pour into a wine glass.

Tom And Jerry

Brandy	½ oz
Rum	½ oz

Place a sugar cube into a water glass, add some hot milk and both of the ingredients into the glass and stir. Top with a sprinkle of nutmeg powder.

Cherry Brandy

Cherry juice	200 ml
Brandy	4.5 L
Sugar	250 g

Add all the ingredients into a large jar and mix, seal and keep it for 50 days. Strain with a paper filter.

Coffee Parfait

Espresso	2 oz
Milk	2 oz
Sugar	1 tsp

Add all the ingredients into a mixing glass with 2-3 pieces on ice and stir, pour into a coffee cup.

Tam O' Shanter

Sugar	1 tsp
Brandy	2 oz

Add both of the ingredients into a pot, add 350 ml of stout and put it on the heat. Pour into a wine glass and top with a sprinkle of nutmeg powder.

Night Cap

Egg yolk	1 egg
Anisette	1 oz
Curacao	1 oz
Brandy	1 oz

Add all the ingredients into a cocktail shaker with 2-3 pieces of ice and shake well, pour into a wine glass.

Grape juice Highball

Add 2 oz of grape fruit juice into a water glass half-filled with ice, top up with soda water.

Magnolia

Sugar syrup .... 1 tsp
Curacao........... .... 1 tsp
Egg yolk .... 1 egg
Brandy............................. 2 oz

Add all the ingredients into a cocktail shaker half-filled with ice and shake well. Pour into a champagne glass and top up with chilled champagne.

Manhattan Fraser

Egg white .... egg
Italian Vermouth .... 1 oz
Absinthe .... 1 oz

Add all the ingredients into a cocktail shaker half-filled with ice and shake well. Pour into a water glass and add a splash of soda water.

Fraser

Sugar .... ½ tsp
Egg................................... 1
Brandy............................. 1 oz
Yellow Chartreuse .... ½ oz
Maraschino...................... ½ oz
Absinthe .... 5-6 dashes

Add all the ingredients into a mixing glass with 2-3 pieces of ice and stir well, strain into a water glass.

French Coffee Royal

Hot Black Coffee ....4 oz

Brandy.............................1 oz

Add both of the ingredients into a water glass and stir.

Brain Duster

Gomme syrup ....2 dashes

Absinthe ....2/3 oz

Italian Vermouth ....½ oz

Whisky ....small pour

Add all the ingredients into a punch glass half-filled with ice and stir well. Top up with soda water.

Brandy Scaffa

Maraschino.....................1/3 of a glass

Green Chartreuse..........1/3 of a glass

Brandy ....1/3 of a glass

Pour all the ingredients into a whisky glass softly by following the order of the recipe one after the other to make the layers.

Brandy Soda

Add 2 oz of Brandy into a water glass and top up with soda water.

Brandy Ginger Ale

Add 2 oz of Brandy into a water glass and top up with ginger ale.

Brandy Champarelle Cocktail

Maraschino	¼ of a glass
Orange curacao	¼ of a glass
Chartreuse	¼ of a glass
Brandy	¼ of a glass

Pour all the ingredients into a port wine glass softly by following the order of the recipe one after the other to make the layers. Top with few dashes of Angostura bitters.

Black Stripe

Add 2 oz of Rum and a sugar cube into a water glass, top up with hot water. Garnish with some lemon peel.

Black Up

Angostura bitter	2 dashes
Lime juice	3 dashes
Egg	1
Brandy	4 oz

Add all the ingredients into a cocktail shaker half-filled with ice and shake well, pour into a water glass. Top up with soda water and add some sugar if needed.

Bull's Milk

Brandy	3 oz
Sugar	1 tsp
Milk	180ml

Add all the ingredients into a cocktail shaker with 2-3 pieces of ice and shake well, pour into a water glass. Top with a sprinkle of nutmeg powder and cinnamon powder.

Coffee Black

Chilled coffee	4 oz
Brandy	1 oz

Add both of the ingredients into a water glass with a piece of ice and stir.

Comote Hot

Syrup	1 oz
Egg	1
Curacao	1 oz
Claret	2 oz

Add all the ingredients into a pot with some sugar, put on the heat and stir constantly. Take it off the heat as soon as it starts simmering. Pour into a coffee cup and garnish with some lemon peel.

Colombian Skin (Hot Whisky)

Add 1 oz of whisky and a piece of lemon peel into a water glass, Top up with hot water.

Arch Bishop

Sugar	½ tsp
Lemon juice	¼ lemon
Port wine	2 oz
Jamaican Rum	3 dashes

Add all the ingredients into a punch glass half-filled with ice and stir well, top up with soda water.

Cider Nectar

Mitsuya Cider	1/3 bottle
Brandy	½ oz
Sherry	½ oz
Sugar	1 tsp

Add all the ingredients into a punch glass half-filled with ice, stir well and top up with soda water.

Kiss Me Quick

Angostura bitter	2 dashes
Curacao	4 dashes
Absinthe	2 oz

Add all the ingredients into a water glass with 2-3 pieces of ice, top up with soda water and serve with a straw.

Cyprus

Lemon juice	small amount
Egg white	1 egg
Brandy	1 ½ oz
Sugar	1 tsp

Add all the ingredients into a cocktail shaker half-filled with ice and shake well, pour into a wine glass and top with a sprinkle of nutmeg powder.

Gin Pole

Dry Gin	1 oz
Milk	5 oz
Sugar	½ tsp

Add all the ingredients into a cocktail shaker half-filled with ice and shake well, pour into a water glass and top up with soda water.

September Morn

Egg white	1 egg
Lemon juice	½ lemon
Grenadine	½ tsp
Bacardi	3 oz

Add all the ingredients into a cocktail shaker and shake well, pour into a wine glass.

Sherry Bitter

Angostura bitter............3 dashes
Lemon juice.... ....small amount

Add both of the ingredients into a sherry glass, top up with sherry.

Spider

Angostura bitter............2 dashes
Curacao...........................2 dashes
Italian Vermouth...........1/3 oz
Whisky.......... ....2/3 oz

Add all the ingredients into a cocktail shaker half-filled with ice and shake well, pour into a wine glass. Garnish with a maraschino cherry.

$\mathcal{I}$ndex

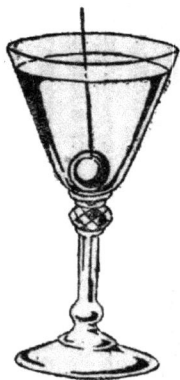

To Our Readers

Finding and translating Kokuteeru (1924) was a year long journey that helps to answer the question "who wrote the first Japanese cocktail book?" Whilst this honour goes to Tokuzo Akiyama's book *Cocktails: How To Mix Drinks*, Yonekichi Maeda's *Kokuteeru* is considered to be the more systematic and practical text which was published a month later. Western style spirits and bartending made their way into Japanese culture as early as 1872. And by the early 1900s Japanese bartenders ran their own Western style establishments. *Kokuteeru* gives us a fascinating glimpse as to how 1920s Japanese bartenders began to define themselves and their profession.

The entirety of the net profits—100%— from the publication of this English translation of *Kokuteeru* will fund the Yonekichi Maeda Scholarship: an internship program that will send Australian bartenders to Japan to learn about Japanese bartending. This scholarship will allow the next generation of Australian bartenders to learn the art of Japanese cocktail bartending and will promote a return of the 'journeyman bartender' to the education scheme of the bartending profession.

In ages past, bartenders travelled to cities around the world to hone their craft. When the enlightened journeyman bartender returned home, this knowledge was shared, enriching both the community and the bartending profession. I believe there is still great value in this idea. And I hope to promote its return.

—Brendan Scott Grey, Perth, Western Australia.

www.ingramcontent.com/pod-product-compliance
Lightning Source LLC
Chambersburg PA
CBHW030105070426
42448CB00037B/980